The Cancer Ethics:

A Radical New Approach to a Medical Mysteries

By

Walter L. Tudor

TABLE OF CONTENT

CHAPTER 1

Understanding Cancer from Antiquity to the Present

The First Accounts of Cancer

Humans and other animals have suffered from cancer throughout recorded history. It is therefore no surprise that since the dawn of history people have been writing about cancer. Some of the earliest evidence of cancer is found among fossil bone tumors, ancient Egyptian mummies, and ancient manuscripts. Growths suggestive of bone cancer called osteosarcoma have been observed in mummies. Cranial destruction, as seen in head and neck cancer, has also been observed. Our oldest description of cancer (although the word cancer is not used) is found in Egypt and dates back to around 3000 BC. It is called the Edwin Smith Papyrus and is a copy of part of the ancient Egyptian manual on trauma surgery. It describes eight cases where breast lumps or sores were removed by cauterization with a tool called a fire drill. The Bible says of this disease: "There is no cure."

Origin of The Word Cancer

The origin of the word cancer is attributed to the Greek physician Hippocrates (460-370 BC), considered the "father of medicine". Hippocrates used the terms carcinoma and carcinoma to describe non-ulcerative and non-ulcerative tumors. In Greek, these words refer to a crab, most likely applied to illness because the finger-like images of cancer resemble the shape of a crab. The Roman physician Celsus (25

BC - 50 AD) later translated the Greek term into cancer, the Latin word for

crab. Galen (AD 130-200), another Greek physician, used the word once (Greek for swelling) to describe tumors. Although Hippocrates and

Celsus' crab analogy is still used to describe malignancies, Galen's term is now used as part of the name of oncologists - oncologists.

Cancer In The 16th-18th Centuries

During the Renaissance, which began in the 15th century, scientists developed a better understanding of the human body. Scientists like Galileo and Newton began using the scientific method, which was later used to study disease. The autopsies, performed by Harvey (1628), led to an understanding of the circulation of blood in the heart and body which until then remained a mystery.

In 1761, Giovanni Morgagni of Padua was the first to do what has become common practice today - he performed autopsies to link a patient's illness to postmortem pathological findings. This laid the foundation for the science of oncology, the study of cancer.

Famous Scottish surgeon John Hunter (1728-1793) suggested that some cancers can be cured by surgery and explained how surgeons can decide which cancers to operate on. If the tumor has not invaded nearby tissue and is "motile," "it is not appropriate to remove it," he said.

A century later, the development of anesthesia made surgery flourish, leading to the development of classic cancer surgeries such as radical mastectomy.

19th-Century Cancer

The 19th century saw the birth of scientific oncology, the study of diseased tissue using modern microscopes. Rudolf Virchow often called the founder of cytopathology, provided the scientific basis for modern pathological cancer research. Just as Morgagni related gross necropsy findings to the clinical course of the disease, Virchow related microscopic

pathology to the disease. This method has not only allowed us to better understand cancer damage but has also contributed to the development of cancer surgery. It is now possible to examine body tissue removed by a surgeon and make an accurate diagnosis. A pathologist can also tell the surgeon whether the cancer was completely removed during surgery.

CHAPTER 2

What Is Cancer

Cancer is a group of diseases characterized by the uncontrollable division of aberrant cells with the ability to invade and destroy normal body tissues. Cancer has the potential to spread throughout the body.

Cancer is an umbrella term. It refers to a disorder in which cells multiply and divide uncontrollably as a result of cellular alterations.

Some tumors produce rapid cell growth, whereas others cause delayed cell growth and division. Certain varieties of cancer produce visible growths known as tumors, while B. leukemia does not.

Most somatic cells have distinct roles and a limited lifespan. Cell death, as horrible as it seems, is a natural and useful event known as apoptosis.

A cell is programmed to die so that the body can replace it with a fresher, more functional cell. Cancer cells have components that instruct them to cease dividing and die. Missing, As a result, they build up in the body, taking the oxygen and nutrients that would otherwise feed other cells. Cancer cells can develop tumors, disrupt the immune system, and induce other alterations that impair function.

Cancer cells could start in one part of her body and travel to her lymph nodes. These are immune cell clusters present throughout the body.

Cancer is the world's second greatest cause of death for females. However, advances in cancer screening, therapy, and prevention have resulted in higher survival rates for many cancers.

How Cancer Grows

Cells are the primary building blocks of the human body. Cells divide and expand to produce new cells as the body requires them. Cells normally die when they get too old or damaged. Then new cells replace them.

Cancer develops when this regular mechanism is disrupted by genetic mutations. Tumors arise when these cells clump together. A malignant tumor is just that: malignant. That indicates it has the potential to grow and spread to other places of the body. A benign tumor can develop but does not spread. Some types of cancer do

not create tumors. Leukemia, most kinds of lymphoma, and myeloma are among them.

How Cancer Spreads

Through the circulation or lymphatic system, cancerous cells can spread to different bodily areas. Launch a glossary entry. They may begin to develop into new tumors there.

Cancers are given names based on the location where they originally appeared. For instance, colon cancer with liver metastases or secondaries is referred to as bowel cancer that has progressed to the liver. It isn't referred to as liver cancer. This is so because diseased bowel cells are also present in the liver's cancerous cells. The malignant cells are not those in the liver.

To metastasize, some cells of primary cancer must separate, travel to another part of the body, and start growing there. Cancer cells do not stick together as well as normal cells. It can also produce substances that stimulate movement.

Some cells slough off and enter nearby small lymphatic or blood vessels called capillaries.

Spread Through The Bloodstream

Cancer cells can invade small blood vessels and enter the bloodstream. They are called circulating tumor cells (or CTCs).

Researchers are trying to diagnose cancer using circulating tumor cells instead of tissue samples. They also want to test circulating cancer cells to see if they can predict which treatments will be more effective. increase.

Circulating blood carries cancer cells until they get stuck somewhere. It often blocks very small blood vessels such as capillaries.

Cancer cells must then migrate through the walls of the capillaries into the tissues of nearby organs. Cells can proliferate and form new tumors if:

• Good conditions for growth

• Contains essential nutrients.

This is a rather complicated process and most cancer cells do not survive. Of the thousands of cancer cells that enter the bloodstream, only a few survive to form secondary cancers. Our immune system's white blood cells find and kill some cancer cells. Other cancer cells can be swept away by the fast-flowing blood and killed.

Circulating cancer cells cling to platelets and form clumps to protect themselves to some degree. Platelets are blood cells that help blood clot. This may also help cancer cells invade surrounding tissues.

Spread Through The Lymphatic System

The lymphatic system is a network of tubes and glands in the body that filter fluids and fight infections. It also traps damaged or harmful cells, such as cancer cells.

Cancer cells can enter small lymphatic vessels near the primary tumor and travel to nearby lymph glands. Cancer cells can die in the lymph glands. However, some survive and grow to form tumors in one or more lymph nodes. This is called lymph node metastasis.

CHAPTER 3

Metastatic Cancer

Metastatic cancer is cancer that has spread from the part of the body where it began (the primary site) to other parts of the body. Once cancer cells separate from a tumor, they can travel through the bloodstream and lymphatic system to other parts of the body. (Lymphatic vessels are very similar to blood vessels, except that they carry clear fluid and cells of the immune system.)

As cells travel through the lymphatic system, they can end up in nearby lymph nodes (clusters of immune cells the size of a pea) or spread to other organs. More commonly, cancer cells away from the primary tumor migrate through the bloodstream. Once in the blood, it can travel to any part of the body. Many of these cells die, but some settle in new areas and start growing.

It takes several steps for cancer cells to spread to new parts of the body:

- They must find a way to separate from the original tumor and enter the bloodstream or lymphatic system.

-

- They must adhere to the walls of blood vessels or lymph vessels and travel to new parts of the body.

- They must find a way to grow and thrive in their new location.

- They must be able to avoid attack by the body's immune system.

Even when cancer spreads to new areas, it is named after the part of the body where cancer originated. For example, breast cancer that has spread to the lung is called "metastatic breast cancer to the lung" and is not lung cancer. Treatment also depends on where the cancer started. If prostate cancer spreads to the bone, it is still prostate cancer (not bone cancer), and your doctor will choose treatments that have been shown to help prevent metastatic prostate cancer. Similarly, colon cancer that has spread to the liver is treated as metastatic colon cancer, not liver cancer.

Metastatic tumors may already have begun to grow when cancer is first detected. Also, metastases may be found before the original (primary) tumor is found. It may be difficult to determine where the cancer is if it has already spread to other parts of the body before it was first diagnosed.

CHAPTER 4

Diagnosing Cancer

Diagnosis often begins when people see a doctor for unusual symptoms. The doctor will discuss the patient's medical history and symptoms. Doctors then perform various tests to find out the cause of these symptoms.

However, many cancer patients are asymptomatic. These people are diagnosed with cancer during a medical examination for another problem or condition. Doctors may find cancer in otherwise healthy people as a result of screening tests. Examples of screening tests are colonoscopy, mammography, and Pap test. Additional tests may be required to confirm or refute the screening test results.

For most cancers, a biopsy is the only way to make a definitive diagnosis. A biopsy is the removal of a small amount of tissue for further examination. Learn more about post-biopsy diagnosis here.

Cancer Symptoms

Because cancer is a small collection of cells, it initially causes no symptoms (see also Overview of Cancer). As cancer grows, its physical presence can affect nearby

tissues (see also Warning Signs of Cancer). Some cancers secrete certain substances or trigger an immune response that causes symptoms in other parts of the body that are not near cancer (paraneoplastic syndromes).

The first indication may be an abnormal laboratory test result for another reason (e.g. anemia due to colon cancer detected on a routine complete blood count). Cancer can invade or press on nearby tissue, affecting nearby tissue, and causing inflammation and compression. Irritation usually causes pain. Compression can prevent the tissue from performing normal functions. For example, bladder cancer or cancerous lymph nodes in the abdomen can compress the tubes that connect the kidneys to the bladder (ureters), blocking the flow of urine. Lung cancer can block airflow through part of the lung, causing partial lung collapse and predisposing to infection. If cancer grows in areas with a lot of space B. In the walls of the colon or lung cavities, it may not cause symptoms until it is quite large. Crabs, by contrast, grow in confined spaces. B. In the vocal cords, causing symptoms (such as hoarseness) when relatively small. Eventually, when cancer spreads (metastasizes) to other parts of the body, it produces the same local irritation and compression effects, but in the new location as such, symptoms can be very different.

Cancers that involve the membrane that covers the lungs (pleura) or the sac that surrounds the heart (pericardium) often ooze fluid that collects around these organs. A large accumulation of fluid can interfere with breathing and the pumping function of the heart.

Pain

Many cancers are usually painless at first, but pain may be an early symptom of some cancers, Pain c be caused by cancer compressing or invading nerves or other structures. However, not all types of cancer cause severe pain. Similarly, the absence of pain is no guarantee that cancer will not grow or spread.

Bleeding

Crabs have fragile blood vessels, so they bleed easily at first. As cancer then spreads and invades surrounding tissue, it can grow into nearby blood

vessels and cause bleeding. Bleeding may be light and undetectable, or it may be detected only by testing. This is common in early-stage colon cancer. Or, especially in advanced

cancer, bleeding can become increasingly heavy and life-threatening. The location of cancer determines the location of the bleeding. Cancer anywhere in the digestive tract may cause bleeding in the stool. Cancer along the urinary tract can cause bleeding in the urine. Other types of cancer can bleed into internal areas of the body. Bleeding into the lungs can cause hemoptysis.

Blood Clots

Certain types of cancer produce substances that cause excessive clot formation, mainly in the leg veins (deep vein thrombosis). A blood clot in a leg vein can rupture and travel to the lungs (pulmonary embolism), which can be fatal. Excessive clotting is common in people with pancreatic, lung, and other solid tumors, and people with brain tumors.

Weight Loss And Fatigue

Cancer patients typically experience weight loss and fatigue, which can get worse as cancer progresses. Some people have big appetites but are skinny. Others may lose their appetite, feel nauseous when eating, or even have difficulty swallowing. Patients with advanced cancer are often very tired. As anemia progresses, even minimal activity can make people feel tired and short of breath.

Swollen Lymph Nodes

When cancer spreads throughout the body, it first spreads to nearby lymph nodes, causing them to swell. Swollen lymph nodes are usually painless and may feel hard or rubbery. They are mobile and if the cancer is more advanced, they stick to the surrounding tissue or stick to each other.

Neurological And Muscular Symptoms

Cancer can invade or press on nerves and the spinal cord, causing a variety of neurological and muscle symptoms, such as pain, muscle weakness, and changes in sensation (such as tingling). When cancer grows in the brain, symptoms can be difficult to identify but may include confusion, dizziness, headache, nausea, blurred vision, and seizures. Neurologic symptoms may also be part of the paraneoplastic syndrome.

Respiratory Symptoms

Cancer can compress or block the airways in the lungs, causing shortness of breath, coughing, or pneumonia. Shortness of breath can also occur if cancer causes a large pleural effusion, bleeding into the lungs, or anemia.

CHAPTER 5

Nutrition And Cancer

The foods we eat can affect our risk of developing certain types of cancer. Eating a high-calorie, high-fat diet can lead to obesity and is generally thought to increase the risk of cancer Eating a variety of nutritious foods can help prevent cancer, as outlined in the Australian Dietary Guidelines. Eating a wide variety of foods from each of the five food groups in recommended amounts contributes to a healthy and interesting diet and provides the body with a wide variety of nutrients. help reduce the risk of diseases. The five food groups are:

- fruits
- Vegetables and legumes/legumes
- Red meat and poultry, fish, eggs, tofu, nuts and seeds, legumes/legumes
- Grain foods, mainly whole grains and/or high fiber varieties
- Milk, yogurt, cheese, and other food substitutes, mainly cut down on fat.

Foods are grouped because they provide similar amounts of important nutrients. For example, the most important nutrients in milk, yogurt, cheese, and alternative food groups include calcium and protein. These food groups make up the Australian Healthy Eating Guide. Diet is just one of the lifestyle factors that influence cancer risk. Smoking, obesity, alcohol, sunbathing and physical activity are also important. Although some foods can affect cancer risk, there is no evidence that any particular food causes or cures cancer.

Grains Prevent Cancer

Consuming seven or more servings of a variety of grains, cereal products, legumes, roots, and tubers daily also protects against cancer. Less processed grains are better, so aim for whole grains. Oats, brown rice, corn, rye, kidney beans, and lentils are good foods. Diets high in refined starches and refined sugars may increase the risk of stomach and colon cancer.

Meat And Colon Cancer

There is now compelling scientific evidence that eating processed meat increases the risk of colon cancer. The World Cancer Research Fund (WCRF) recently recommended avoiding eating processed meat. Processed meat includes all meat that has been cured, cured, smoked, or preserved by the addition of chemical

preservatives. This includes hot dogs, ham, bacon, sausages, and hamburgers. We recommend not giving your child processed meat. This is because many of the habits we develop as children continue into adulthood. Recommended processed meat substitutes for children include fish, lean poultry, lean meats, and low-fat cheeses. There is compelling evidence that red meat also increases the risk of colon cancer. People, especially men, are encouraged to reduce their consumption of red meat. It is recommended that you limit it to some studies that suggest that eating charred or charred meat may increase the risk of cancer, but the evidence is unclear. The Australian Healthy Eating Guide recommends eating a variety of foods from the "lean meats and nuts and seeds and legumes and legumes" food group.

Fat And Cancer

There has been much interest in the possible link between fat and cancer. Current evidence does not suggest a direct link between fat intake and specific cancers (with the possible exception of prostate cancer). However, a high-fat diet can lead to obesity and is a risk factor for several cancers, including those of the colon, breast, kidney, esophagus, gallbladder, and endometrial lining.

Fruits, Vegetables, And Cancer

It has long been known that eating fruits and vegetables has many health benefits. Fruits and vegetables are rich in vitamins, minerals, and antioxidants that help reduce the risk of cancer in certain areas of the digestive system, such as the mouth and stomach. Evidence for the role of fruits and vegetables in cancer prevention has weakened in recent years. However, fruits and vegetables are still an important part of the diet, relatively low in kilojoules (energy), and eating them is associated with a healthy weight, which may indirectly help prevent cancer.

CHAPTER 6

Common Cancers And Foods

Some common cancers can be affected by diet, including lung cancer, breast cancer, prostate cancer, and colon cancer.

Lung Cancer

Lung cancer is the leading cause of cancer-related deaths worldwide and most lung cancers are caused by smoking. A healthy diet high in fruits and vegetables is associated with a lower risk of lung cancer in both smokers and nonsmokers. Recent evidence suggests that cruciferous vegetables such as cabbage, cauliflower, broccoli, and bok choy are excellent vegetable choices. Eating fruits and vegetables may provide some protection against lung cancer but quitting smoking (and avoiding second-hand smoke) is the best prevention.

Breast Cancer

Breast cancer is the most common type of cancer in women worldwide. Factors such as rapid premature growth, height in adulthood, and weight gain in adulthood increase the risk of breast cancer. Much of the risk of developing breast cancer is associated with factors that affect estrogen levels in a woman's reproductive life. For example, age at menarche (first menstrual period), delay in menopause, number of pregnancies, delay in a first pregnancy, and breastfeeding habits. The incidence of breast cancer also increases with age. A postmenopausal woman who is overweight, especially in midlife, has an average risk of breast cancer more than double that of her. A diet high in monounsaturated fats, such as olive oil, canola oil, and some nuts and seeds, and high in vegetables may reduce

the risk. Consuming large amounts of alcohol may increase the risk of breast cancer.

Prostate Cancer

Prostate cancer is the most common type of cancer in Australian men. Men over the age of 50 are at increased risk. But it is also found in young men. Vegetables (especially soybeans) may reduce the risk, but a high-fat diet consisting primarily of animal fat sources (dairy products, fatty meats, take-out, etc.) may increase the risk. Maintaining a healthy weight can reduce the risk of prostate cancer. Lycopene is a

Powerful antioxidants are found in tomatoes, tomato-based products, watermelon, and strawberries and may help reduce the risk of prostate cancer. 1/2 cup or 75 grams per serving), there is evidence to reduce the risk of prostate cancer.

Colon Cancer

Colorectal cancer (colon cancer) is the second leading cause of cancer-related deaths in Australia. Up to 70% of cases can be prevented with a healthy lifestyle. Maintaining a healthy weight, exercising, and eating a diet high in vegetables and fiber can protect your body, but eating large amounts of red meat, processed meat, and alcohol can increase your risk.

Cancer Protection - Limit Food And Drink

Foods and drinks that restrict or reduce eating include:

• Fatty red meat and processed meat

• Highly processed foods low in fiber

• Salty foods and pickles

• Alcohol.

Protection Against Cancer – "Eat More" Foods.

The strongest protective anti-cancer effects are shown below.

• Vegetables, especially green leafy vegetables, raw vegetables such as carrots, and salads

High fiber foods such as grains and cereals

• tomato

Citrus fruits (oranges, grapefruits, lemons, limes, etc.)

• Cruciferous vegetables such as broccoli, cabbage, Brussels sprouts, bok choy, and other Asian vegetables. Incorporate these vegetables and fruits into your diet along with other varieties.

Dietary supplements are not the answer to cancer prevention

The World Cancer Research Fund suggests that high-dose supplements are not recommended for cancer prevention and that the best approach to cancer prevention is to meet nutritional needs with whole foods.

Studies may show that foods containing certain nutrients have protective effects. However, this does not mean that these nutrients provide the same cancer-preventing benefits as when taken as a dietary supplement.

In some cases, cancer risk is increased in people taking dietary supplements at higher than normal amounts of this nutrient normally found in food. For example, the use of beta-carotene and vitamin E supplements is not effective in preventing or treating lung cancer.

CHAPTER 7

Foods That Increase Cancer Risk

High-energy, low-fiber diets may increase cancer risk, but some individual foods are potentially carcinogenic (can cause cancer).) are classified as This also includes:

Artificial sweeteners – such as aspartame, saccharin, and cyclamate. Lab rats fed high doses of saccharin or cyclamate are 1,000 times more likely to develop bladder cancer than those fed a normal diet. International research shows that people are not affected in the same way. Artificial sweeteners are considered safe

Salted, pickled, or salty foods — Bacon and other salted or pickled foods contain substances called nitrates, which can cause cancer, especially colon cancer, in large amounts. There is nature. For safety reasons, it is recommended that you limit the amount of cured meats in your diet, as cured meats are usually high in fat and salt.

Burnt or Baked Food - A group of carcinogens known as polycyclic aromatic hydrocarbons (PAHs) can be produced when food is overheated or burnt. Burnt and smoked foods may contain trace amounts of PAHs, but experts believe the average Australian diet contains too low levels to be considered a significant cancer risk. I don't think so. I agree that it is not possible. However, when cooking, try to cook at a low temperature as much as possible and avoid meat and charcoal grills. Low-temperature cooking methods include steaming, simmering, simmering, simmering, simmering, baking, broiling, microwaving, and frying.

Peanuts - Some laboratory animals develop cancer after eating peanuts contaminated with toxin-producing molds. However, peanuts sold in Australia are generally uncontaminated and are regularly tested for contamination.

Alcohol - Drinking alcohol increases your risk of mouth, throat, larynx, esophagus, breast, colon, and liver cancer. Smokers are even more at risk. To reduce the risk of illness, a man should drink not more than two drinks a day and a woman should drink no more than one drink a day.

CHAPTER 8

Immunotherapy

Immunotherapy is the latest breakthrough to change and improve the standard of care for cancer treatment. This therapy, combined with clinical therapy, helps the patient use their immune system to fight cancer. Immunotherapy considered a biological therapy, can boost or change the immune system's ability to find and attack cancer cells. As it functions normally, the immune system is a collection of organs and specialized cells that protect you from infection and disease by identifying and destroying abnormal cells. Strengthens the body's natural defenses by training the immune system to do so, resulting in "immune memory." This "immune memory" usually leads to long-lasting remission as the body understands how to deal with most cancer recurrences. Immunotherapies used to treat cancer include:

- Checkpoint inhibitors enable the immune system to initiate a response to cancer cells.
- T-cell transplant therapy This therapy modifies the infection-fighting T cells obtained from the patient's blood and rewrites the blood cells to recognize and attack cancer cells. was once After being rewritten, the blood is returned to the patient's body.
- Monoclonal Antibodies – Artificial versions of immune system proteins that act like the patient's own antibodies to boost the immune system.
- Therapeutic vaccines, such as the human papillomavirus (HPV) vaccine, which helps prevent cervical, vaginal, vulvar, and anal cancer, and the hepatitis B vaccine, which helps prevent liver cancer.

- Immune system modulators – A class of drugs that strengthen parts of the immune system to naturally fight cancer. These immunotherapies are currently being used to treat the below cancers:
- Brain
- Breast
- Cervical
- Colorectal
- Kidney
- Leukemia
- Lung
- Lymphoma
- Melanoma Due to immunotherapy's strong ability to fight cancer using a body's immune system, it is generally compared to chemotherapy and can complement each other. While chemotherapy and immunotherapy can both be used to kill cancer cells, they differ in their approach:

Chemotherapy uses special drugs to kill fast-growing cells, both cancerous and non-cancerous and is generally seen as a reactive approach to cancer.

Immunotherapy uses various drugs and treatments to train your body to combat cancer cells, generally being seen as a preventative or long-term approach to fighting cancer. Chemotherapy and immunotherapy when combined show how they are a powerful force against most cancer cells in your body, then boost the body's natural defenses after the fact. Oncologists and researchers continue to test and practice different treatments to combat cancer and provide additional breakthrough treatments for all cancers. Am Memorial Care Todd Cancer Institute Am Memorial Care.